'THEY' ARE NOT MILLENNIALS

David Brown

Editing: Chris Barsanti

Design and Production: Aaron Farrier

Paradigm Multimedia

For permissions contact:
request@cultureofcommand.com

First printing, November 2019

Library of Congress Control Number: 2019909578

ISBN-13:978-1-7333007-0-4

Published by:
Culture of Command, LLC
www.cultureofcommand.com

Dedicated to you, for actively studying leadership.

CONTENTS

Introduction

As with any leadership book, this book exists to give the reader the tools to successfully lead a group of people. It explicitly intends to examine and understand the next generation of employees and future leaders in the post-Millennial generation, or what researchers are starting to call "Generation Z."

One of the first things you may have noticed about this book is its length. In today's fast-paced, technologically-enhanced environment, the need to quickly disseminate information is more important than ever before. As you read through this book, you will learn that the younger generation values speed of information sharing more than any prior generation. As the world gets faster and faster, we must lead by example and tailor our messages to facilitate brief information sharing. We must be concise and say more with less. Think of the world we live in as a series of tweets—limited to 140 characters per statement. But only nine percent of tweets ever hit the 140-character count, with an average tweet length of 34 characters. When Twitter expanded their character limit to 280 characters per tweet, the average tweet length decreased to 33 characters.[1] This illustrates Generation Z's preference for quick-hitting information dissemination.

This book also exists because of personal experience. I have seen many leaders and managers crumble while trying to find a solution to lead, motivate, and inspire an increasingly young workforce.

As I was sitting in a leadership class, I started noticing trends in my classmates. Everyone in the room was already in a leadership position; these were considered the best and brightest of their organizations, the up-and-comers. As the class settled in, the instructor displayed a slide from his

---

[1] **Perez, Sarah. 2018**. "Twitter's doubling of character count from 140 to 280 had little impact on length of tweets." *TechCrunch*. Accessed March 26, 2019. techcrunch.com/2018/10/30/twitters-doubling-of-character-count-from-140-to-280-had-little-impact-on-length-of-tweets/.

PowerPoint presentation. We were instructed to stand up and introduce ourselves to one another by following the displayed prompts:

- What is your name?
- How long have you been in a leadership position?
- What are your hobbies?
- What do you most want to get out of this class?

As I sat back and listened to my new classmates share their leadership experiences, I began to notice a trend. My classmates were a collective group of "go-getters," put into formal leadership positions to guide the next generation of workers. The average age of the class was 42 years old. Soon, another trend arose. Each classmate began to answer the last question in a very familiar way:

- "I don't know how to deal with these kids."
- "Millennials only seem to want to take vacations. I can't seem to get them to put in the hours."
- "They don't respond to my emails or texts."
- "These Millennials want instant gratification. They don't want to be here. They don't value working

hard for what they want."

The gripes and complaints continued. Even the instructor joined in. The instructor spoke about how Millennials "confuse" him and how he "doesn't understand" what their issues are. He then reassured the class his course would offer insight on how to "deal" with Millennials.

Aside from the fact that as a leader, you do not "deal" with a group of people, an even more glaring issue came to mind. This was a course devoted to leadership and attended by leaders. Yet, nobody seemed to have an answer to the millennial question. It was as if all the leaders and managers in the course were throwing their hands in the air and giving up. They committed one of the biggest mistakes of leadership: giving up on their people.

To further complicate matters, the sentiments shared by the attendees, even the instructor, as to what they view as being the critical issues with Millennial employees, didn't actually describe the Millennial generation at all. These leaders were trying to solve a generational gap in their work groups by falling back on the "Millennial" buzzword that had been used by leaders and corporate heads preceding them.

Sure, you can Google "leadership tactics for Millennials" and the search engine will populate a plethora of suggestions on how to manage the Millennials, but it won't complete the picture.

According to the Pew Research Group, the first wave of Millennials were born in 1981[2]. That means that in 2019, the oldest Millennials turn 38 years old. In every conference, meeting, and training session I have attended, I have heard almost every negative trait of the Millennial generation. We see it on the news, we complain about them to our co-workers, we silently judge them in line at the local coffee shop. Given that the oldest Millennials are nearing 40, it stands to reason that a number of Millennials are now leaders in their organizations. For a large number of people reading this book; "we" are Millennials.

In hearing about Millennials and how they are an incredibly hard group of people to manage, I quickly came to the realization that people weren't complaining about

---

[2] **Pew Research Center: Internet and Technology. (2014).** "Part 1: How the internet has woven itself into American life." Accessed March 26, 2019. https://www.pewinternet.org/2014/02/27/part-1-how-the-internet-has-woven-itself-into-american-life/.

38-year-olds. They weren't looking at the employee in their early 30s and trying desperately to lead or manage them. The "they" being complained about was something much different.

"They" are not Millennials.

The infamous "they" that everyone was trying to learn how to motivate, was a group distinctly different from Millennials. The employees in question were in fact an even younger generation; referred to as Generation-Z, iGen, or even Post-Millennials.

By making this misassumption at the onset, these leaders were failing from the start. They were trying to lead a generation of people they did not know. Not only did these leaders not know anything about Generation Z, they were also wrong in identifying them. Their current approach would be similar to treating a cold by using a Band-Aid. It just won't work.

A new approach is necessary. The first step is identifying the correct subject of these complaints, then formulating a strategy based on that understanding.

Understand.

CHAPTER ONE
Understand.

One of the most critical components of leadership is understanding who you are intending to lead. For Generation Z, we must understand that they are not the same as Millennials. While there are many similarities to the Millennial generation, Generation Z is a distinctly different group of people. Understanding that the youngest employees are different from Millennials is the first step to being able to successfully lead, motivate, and inspire Generation Z.

While researchers are still studying the inherent traits of Generation Z, its oldest members have started to enter the workforce. Managers, supervisors, and leaders have already noticed differences in "the new generation." The goal of this section is to gain an understanding of

Generation Z. Leading and influencing Generation Z requires understanding Generation Z. You do not need to agree with them. You do not need to become them. However, you need to understand them.

Leadership requires a fundamental understanding of human behavior. Understanding human behavior allows you to predict human behavior. If you can understand how an employee thinks, as well as why they feel the way they do, you can more easily empathize and influence outcomes.

CHAPTER TWO
Defining Generation Z

In keeping with the idea of understanding Generation Z, let's start at the beginning. They were born approximately around 1995. There is no exact science as to a hard line date and time that a person is defined in one generation or the next. With that being said, most research indicates that the oldest members of Generation Z will be approximately 25 years old in 2019.

Generation Z'ers are the digital pioneers. In 1995, roughly 14 percent of adults had access to the internet. By 2014, 87 percent of adults had that same access.[3] All of a

---

3

Pew Research Center: Internet and Technology. (2014). "Part 1: How the internet has woven itself into American life." Accessed

sudden, the world became much smaller and more accessible. Instead of using pen pals to gain knowledge and to share experiences, the Gen Z'ers could utilize messaging services, such as AOL Instant Messenger (R.I.P.).

Generation Z is the first generation to come of age in a society with a strong social media presence. The Millennials might have experienced the internet boom and the birth of social media, but the oldest of them only saw Facebook emerge as they were graduating college. Generation Z grew up in the era of Facebook, Instagram, Snapchat, and other social media platforms. This access to social media, and the speed at which news is disseminated, has profoundly impacted them as a generation. Millennials were thought to have a short attention span, 12 seconds on average. Generation-Z, on the other hand, has a shorter attention span of approximately eight seconds. [4]

March 26, 2019.https://www.pewinternet.org/2014/02/27/part-1-how-the-internet-has-woven-itself-into-american-life/.

[4] **Brenner, Michael. 2014**. "Thanks Social Media - Our Average Attention Span Is Now Shorter Than Goldfish." Marketing Insider Group. Accessed March 26, 2019. https://

Attention span is not the only thing affected by the increasing speed of society. Generation-Z members are incredible multitaskers. They are superiorly capable of processing multiple bits of information simultaneously, albeit eight seconds at a time. They receive Twitter news articles in 140 characters or less. They were accustomed to watching 5-second Vine videos (while it still existed), and they pass information from one another in short bursts. If you have kids, you have probably witnessed this. Trying to keep up on the conversation between two members of Generation Z can be a daunting task. They seem to flow between ideas, topics, and events effortlessly. Additionally, Gen-Z'ers rely heavily on visual aids such as memes to communicate with one another.

That shorter attention span has also led to a considerable shift in how Gen Z'ers interact with the economic landscape. Their shopping trends have pushed companies to innovate across the globe. Two-day shipping seems like an eternity to a person with an 8-second attention span. Many companies are shifting to on-demand

marketinginsidergroup.com/content-marketing/thanks-social-media-average-attention-span-now-shorter-goldfish/

everything. Amazon, in select cities, offers guaranteed two-hour delivery. Convenience is taking precedence over brand names. Retailers are scrambling to keep up with the trends set by Generation Z.

Constant connectivity, has had other impacts on the Gen-Z'ers. They grew up in an era of email, communicating in texts, and substituting language for emojis. The result of this changed the way that they want to interact in the workplace. Surprisingly, Generation-Z employees prefer face-to-face contact over emails. According to research, 74 percent of Gen Z'ers prefer meeting in person[5]. The social connectedness once lost in the Millennials is back with Generation Z. It is easy to dismiss an employee by deleting an email. It is much harder to push back against or ignore a person speaking with you face-to-face in your office. Generation Z knows both the value they possess and that the most accurate way to convey it is in person.

Generation Z does not have the typical kind of celebrities that other generations had. Justin Bieber was a

---

[5] **Lingo Staffing. 2018**. "Generation Z is Here: Is Your Company Ready for the New Kids on the Workforce Block?" Accessed March 26, 2019. https://lingostaffing.com/1091-2/.

Millennial generation celebrity. He doesn't stand a chance when compared to the next social influencer.[6] Instead, they are more likely to value the opinions of real people who are putting out original content across multiple social media platforms. The idea that a non-famous person, just like them, could buy, review, and post the opinions of an item is alluring. It also points to something much more profound; Gen Z'ers value genuine feedback. They don't want to be lied to by anybody, not even a celebrity selling the next most excellent product. They value real information in real time.

Along with social influencers, who create content and publish it for the world to see, Gen Z'ers are incredibly entrepreneurial.[7] The idea that they can start and run their

---

[6] **Geyser, Werner. 2019.** "Why YouTube Stars are More Influential than Traditional Celebrities." Influencer Marketing Hub. Accessed March 26, 2019. https://influencermarketinghub.com/youtube-stars-influential-traditional-celebrities/..

[7] **Gallup, Inc. 2016.** "2017 National Scorecard." Accessed March 26, 2019. http://www.gallupstudentpoll.com/197492/2016-national-scorecard.aspx.

own companies is driving many of them to change the way in which they view education, as well as, career paths. The traditional method of going to college, gaining debt, and working a job they may not like, is changing. With the advent of digital publishing and the teaching mechanisms of YouTube, Generation Z is challenging the standard approach to life and career.

With the entrepreneurial spirit comes an additional preference. Generation Z, completely opposite from the Millennial generation, prefers to work solo.[8] They view their work function as a part of a more extensive system, preferring individual workspaces, but also desiring to know that their work fits into a more significant role. It is the idea of knowing how the "widget" they produce fits into the final product. Autonomy to make decisions and implement policy changes are highly valued traits in their workplace.

As demonstrated by news headlines, you know that Get

---

[8] **Gelber, Mack. 2016**. "Here's what you need to know about Gen Z, boss." **Monster Career Advice.** Accessed March 26, 2019. https://www.monster.com/career-advice/article/gen-z-boss-0816

Z'ers are incredibly optimistic.[9] They started anti-bullying campaigns and ditched the 'Mean-Girls' persona of the past. Instead, they focus on supporting one another, building positive body images with each other and uplifting the emotional state of everyone with which they come into contact. It is an incredible thing to turn on the news and see teenagers standing up for what they consider right and just in the world.

It doesn't stop there; this trait is continued well into college and in the workplace. Members of Generation-Z are constantly looking for ways to improve the world. Because they view problems as a function of the larger society, they want to address root causes, not just address symptoms.

Moving forward, will look at how Generation-Z experienced their formative years and how that affects their thinking. Thought processes we will examine what allows them to thrive in the workplace as well as how to

---

[9] **Turner, Marcia Layton. (2018).** "How Generation Z Views the Future: A Word on Optimism." *Spark.* Accessed March 26, 2019. https://www.adp.com/spark/articles/2018/12/how-generation-z-views-the-future-a-word-on-optimism.aspx#

lead them in the future.

Review: Defining Generation Z?

- Access to a lot of information - grew up in the digital age.

- Will process things very quickly.

- Great at multi-tasking.

- Place value on 'Social Influencers.'

- Have an 8-second attention span.

- Incredibly optimistic.

- Strong desire to be entrepreneurs.

- Altruistic / Accepting of others.

Lead.

CHAPTER THREE
Communication

Now that we have reviewed the origins of Generation-Z, we can begin to translate that knowledge into a leadership style that precisely suits their characteristics. The frequency in which you meet with your employees and how you communicate with them are linked to the morale of your workforce. Generation Z is a generation that grew up with social media, providing instant feedback. According to research provided by The Center For Generational Kinetics, 60% of Generation Z employees prefer more communication and feedback from their employers.

One of the hardest things to learn as a leader is how to effectively communicate with the next generation. Far too often, I've seen leaders and managers lecture to employees of Generation Z. This style of communication may have been sufficient for Generation X, and perhaps even some Millennials, however, with an 8-second attention span, this style will not suffice for Generation-Z employees. Additionally, Generation Z employees respond better if communication occurs face-to-face. Gen Z'ers tend to feel that tone, intent, and contextual clues of effective communication are missing in emails and texts.

When discussing work performance with Generation Z, the conversation is much more concise. Five years ago, the conversation would have extended to beyond 30 minutes. Today however, given how quickly Generation Z processes information, the employees absorb the information shockingly fast, quickly gathering feedback and preparing to tackle the next task.

One of my managers tried to address an issue that had arisen with a reasonably young employee. The manager spent roughly an hour talking in their office with the employee about a mistake on a project. During that hour, the manager spent approximately 10 minutes discussing the problem at hand, going into depth about where the mistake had been made and also why it was so severe. The remainder of the time was spent discussing the positive things that the employee had done in the past. The manager was trying to convey that he valued the employee. Unfortunately, however, the employee only focused on the content of the first 10 minutes.

Moreover, in the employee's mind the entire hour-long conversation was negative. The employee viewed this as a lecture and felt as if they had been talked down to in that situation. As with any employee, they took their complaints to the break room. Rumors started spreading about how the manager was too critical in his evaluation of situations, and other employees began to talk negatively about the manager.

As the grumbling continued, I knew I had to develop a new system for engaging employees. As I researched effective communication for Generation Z, I quickly learned that while they do prefer face-to-face contact, they more frequently want it kept very brief. As a result, I implemented what is known as the three-sentence rule. This rule is based on the concept of effectively getting a message across as quickly as possible. The idea is to first explain what was wrong and why it was wrong, then show or explain how to fix the issue, and lastly to gather feedback and ask whether the employee has any other questions about the issue.

As we began implementing the three-sentence rule, employees took that as a sign that we, as organizational leaders, are at least hearing them and noticing that they were feeling micromanaged. None of the managers had previously thought they were micromanaging. However, perception is reality. With a shortened attention span, what the manager might have honestly intended as a conversation could feel like a browbeating session to the person on the receiving end.

By changing this one simple technique in how managers talked to their people, the morale of the organization significantly increased. People were friendlier and more open with each other about sharing ideas. It was an adjustment for the managers, as they had to get used to becoming more genuine, to-the-point, directed, and - concise with their message. The flip side was that the new method of communication did not always leave enough to explain precisely why something was wrong and deal with the issue in a substantive manner.

Watching seasoned managers learn to communicate on a different level to reach the people they were leading, it became clear that the change in approach also gave them a sense of hope. While there were naturally still complaints about the next generation of the young people entering the workforce, the managers started to see hope because they were able to communicate more effectively and understand the younger employees' ideas.

If effective communication does not exist within your organization, you will struggle to lead your people effectively. In order to influence someone, it is critical that you are able to convey to them what it is you want them to do. If this kind of communication is impossible, it becomes a very frustrating process on both sides of the message.

The most critical takeaway of this section is that when you meet with your employees, keep the meetings brief. Provide positive feedback when warranted and correct other issues by utilization of the three-sentence rule.

Review: Communication tips with Generation - Z:

- Navigate an 8-second attention span.

- Meet face to face.

- Provide frequent feedback.

- Be genuine and concise.

Embrace the 'Three Sentence Rule':

- This is what is wrong.

- This is how you fix it.

- Any questions?

CHAPTER FOUR
Tough Talks

Being a leader requires more than the ability to manage resources. Being a leader necessitates being a guide for your employees. At times that requires having tough talks with your employees. Frank discussions, while uncomfortable, are vital to helping your employees grow in their personal or professional development.

The tough talks you initiate, if done correctly, will help employees take a reflective look at their performance and the direction in which they are heading. The most uncomfortable moments of your career may end up yielding the most growth. Given how frequently Generation-Z wants to be communicated with, they prefer it to be genuine. Keep in mind that, given the fast-paced environment which the younger workforce has grown accustomed to, wasting time by not getting to the point could be a detriment.

Start with a goal in mind

Before beginning your tough talk, plan out where you want the conversation to go, especially if you are addressing a performance issue. When your end goal is to make the employee perform better, your communication will cater towards building a person up. Ending on highlighting positive results will make your employee feel safe in their career. Failure to do so will make it look as if you are merely attacking a person. Remember, offer solutions rather than just bringing up problems. We tend to assume younger workers need the "kid glove" treatment. That isn't necessarily the case. A younger workforce may be experiencing adversity for the first time, at a transitional time of their lives. Taking the time to consider outside factors is merely doing what we should do for every employee, regardless of age.

Be specific with examples

It is very frustrating to endure a conversation in which

someone is criticizing your work, actions, or thought processes but has no specific examples of these deficiencies. If you critique someone for having a poor work performance, be sure to cite what makes the work product substandard.

Think back to a time when a supervisor came to talk with you. The issue at hand may have been a minor detail in the grand scheme of things. Think of how you were approached and how the different approaches resonated with you. When a person with perceived authority only discusses general gripes or complaints, their perceived credibility wanes. For example, if you have ever been told that you had terrible customer service skills, was it backed up with specific examples? If not, there is a good chance that you took the conversation personally. If an employee receives a message like this as a personal attack, they likely will not listen to anything further that the supervisor has to say.

Address issues promptly

If you recognize that an issue developing, do not let it fester. Address it quickly, do not allow it to become acceptable performance or a bad habit. Additionally, if you are meeting with someone to discuss an issue, jump right in. Don't sit around and circle the subject while making small talk. Chances are, the employee likely knows that they are deficient in some manner; killing time adds to the recipients anxiety.

Even if the issues being discussed are not specific to the person with whom you are talking, it is essential that people trust you will take action when needed. In addition to wanting fast communication and ideas to flow, younger employees also value a stress-free work life.

Point out good deeds

In addition to reprimanding, there must be a building phase. Undoubtedly, each member of your team has many good qualities. Professional or personal, there is something about that individual that got him or her the job. Find that quality and build upon it.

Advocating for one another is commonplace in the current culture. People build each other up and give each other the confidence they may have lacked themselves. This is a recurring theme with younger social media users.

These talks are far different from constantly telling people how great they are without a reality check. This is merely delivering the "reality check" while simultaneously showing that you value a person.

I am sure that at some point in our professional lives, each of us has left a meeting feeling like we should pack our office. We may have felt devalued. The distractions and the sense of inadequacy that can come along with that feeling are counterproductive to work productivity and can impact the culture of an entire organization.

Similarly to being specific to examples of workplace deficiencies, be specific with exceptional performance. We tend, as people to focus on the negative, look for the positive in your employees. Find them doing something right. Document their great work effort or product and make sure your employees know that you notice their good deeds.

Develop a plan

Having a plan in place is paramount. As a leader, it is unacceptable for you to identify performance issues, discuss them, and dismiss the employee back to their normal routine. For an employee to grow, you must develop the plan of action for or with them. You likely have the experience or resources to help each employee be successful. Garner input from the person having the issue and before the end of the meeting make sure there is a plan in place to rectify any problem presented.

Sometimes a program may be as simple as adding a training session into the development plan to ensure your employees understand their roles and expectations. Other times it may be something much more complex, involving numerous follow-up meetings and enacting specific deadlines.

When developing a plan for your employee, ensure first and foremost it is reasonable. The plan must be something they can follow and adhere to given their skill-set. Your plans must be laid out appropriately to ensure the employee knows exactly what is being measure of them and the frequency in which it will be measured.

A common workplace problem with employees is proper time management. An example of a developmental plan to assist with time management would simply be for the employee to document their daily routine. Document their time spent on tasks. Bring an awareness to the employees daily routine. The employee should not be expected to continue this practice for a lengthy period of time. Perhaps 2-weeks or up to one-month will suffice. Correct the action and move on.

Too often, I hear of leaders addressing issues with their team, yet offering no solution on how to rectify the fundamental deficiencies noted. Inaction is itself an action, and if you care for your people and want to lead them to success, it requires work on your part.

Review: Handling a Tough Talk:

- *Start with an end-goal in mind.*

- *Cite specific examples.*

- *Don't let issues fester, address them promptly.*

- *Point out good deeds, include positive feedback to build upon.*

- *Have and implement a plan to improve.*

CHAPTER FIVE
Retention

Increasingly, the term "start-up" has transitioned from something that sounded foreign to an almost household term. As the next generation of the American workforce has more access to a global economy, it brings a renewed entrepreneurial spirit. In a massive study sponsored by Monster, it was found that nearly half (46 percent) of Generation-Z respondents stated that they wanted to start their own business. That number grows to 72 percent if we factor in high school students who have yet to enter the workforce.[10]

---

[10] **Patel, Deep. 2017**. "How Gen Z Will Affect The Future Of The Peer To Peer Economy." *Forbes*.https://www.forbes.com/sites/deeppatel/2017/08/29/how-gen-z-will-affect-the-future-of-the-peer-to-peer-economy/.

With the young workforces affinity to own their own companies, the question then becomes: How do leaders retain employees? At the heart of that question is the underlying assumption that you want to retain your employees. High turnover is expensive. It causes lag times in production, the personnel hours spent on employee orientation, and the bureaucracy many companies are likely to experience when hiring an employee.

To look at this question from a leadership perspective requires breaking down the situation itself. Regarding employee retention, there are two tracks we need to look at as leaders of Generation-Z:. Administrative Actions (or functions) and Leadership Development Opportunities. When it comes to administrative actions, you, as the formal leader, may not be able to have as much of an impact as you are in the leadership development category. Your level of impact will be directly proportional to your scope of control within the organization. Again, to be able to effectively develop a plan that allows us to lead, motivate, and inspire an individual or group; an essence of understanding is required. The two tracts are found in the

_____

explanation further below.

Administrative Actions

Administrative actions are things that we cannot always control. Pay increases, bonuses, vacation packages, etc. Are all examples of administrative actions. As stated above, depending upon the level of control you may have within your organization, you may or may not be able to alter administrative actions to meet the needs of a Generation-Z employee. Thinking back to the "Understand" section, we observe that members of Generation Z came of age during the housing market collapse and government bailouts. Examining that information through the lens of understanding, we see trends incredibly similar to those seen in the Traditionalist Generation, born between 1922 and 1945 and also known as the "Greatest Generation" for their contributions and sacrifices many made during World War II. For employers, this is information that can be used to your advantage when developing an incentive package worthy of retaining Generation Z.

Similar to the Traditionalists, Generation Z came of age during an economic downturn. Generation Z watched their parents and society struggle to make ends meet. As the financial world collapsed around them, frugality presented itself as a way of life. Banks and auto-manufacturers were being bailed out, and the housing market crashed seemingly overnight. Similarly, the Traditionalists came of age during the Great Depression. While the economic downturn in the mid-2000s was nowhere near as severe as the Great Depression, the impact it had was very real to those who experienced it first-hand[11].

For Generation Z, witnessing the world's financial struggles during their formative years swung the pendulum of importance back to income. Seventy percent of Generation Z stated that their salary was their top career motivator. [12](Monster Career Advice, 2016) This is a shift

---

[11] **Stahl, Ashley. (2017).** "Why Democrats Should be Losing Sleep Over Generation Z. *Forbes.* Accessed March 26, 2019. https://www.forbes.com/sites/ashleystahl/2017/08/11/why-democrats-should-be-losing-sleep-over-generation-z/#55fe57657878

[12] **Gelber, Mack. 2016.** "Here's what you need to know about Gen Z, boss." **Monster Career Advice.** Accessed March 26, 2019. https://www.monster.com/career-advice/article/gen-z-boss-0816

in culture in just one generation. In similar surveys, Millennials responded that their top priorities were flexible working hours or remote work locations[13].

Additionally, seeing the impact that rising health care costs had on their families, Generation Z also listed health benefits as a "must have" seven out of ten times[14].

While you may not have the authority to dictate what types of employer benefits packages are offered, it is essential that you take note of what is available for your workers.

There are other things you can do from your current position to assist in retaining employees.

Leadership Development

To harness that entrepreneurial spirit, remember that 46 percent of current Generation Z employees want to own their own business and that to retain employees we have to look back to understanding that Generation Z is often seeking greater command of their career destiny[15].

---

[13] **Patel, D.**

[14] **Gelber, Mack.**

[15] Patel, D.

As a leader, you are able to nurture and facilitate employees taking charge of their own lives careers. This is accomplished by building the skills of your employees and empowering them to govern their careers. This is not a new concept in leadership, with many volumes dedicated to this exact topic.

One of the easiest ways to engage and empower an employee is to make them a part of the decision-making process. We all want to feel we have a role in the organization. We also want to feel that our opinions matter and that others find value in our existence. Giving ownership of a project to employees is a surefire way to prove you value and have trust in them. Additionally, seeking their input and guidance before a meeting or before making a large-scale organizational decision is another feasible way to include your employees.

When we include others in what is going on around them, they often feel like they are part of the larger organization. Taking pride in ownership and having a say in the direction of their careers may be just the thing your employees need to stay happy and engaged in the workplace.

Similarly to Millennials, Generation-Z wants to

understand the reasons behind what they are being asked to do. Responding with, "We have always done it this way" will not be enough to keep people engaged or help them feel as though they have a part in the organization. More and more, Millennials and Generation-Z want to make impactful decisions at an organizational level. This can be accomplished when a leader takes the time to explain processes and decision-making variables in order to feed their people's strong desire to not only develop themselves but understand the role and purpose of the organization.

Review: Retaining a Gen-Z'er in the workplace:

Understand their background and needs.

- They grew up in an economic downturn.

- They are incredibly inclined to be their own boss.

Meet their needs.

- Offer competitive wages.

- Offer health care.

-Make them part of the decision making process.

- Keep them informed of variables that can affect their careers.

- Value their input and encourage ownership in the organization.

Motivate.

CHAPTER SIX
Motivate.

A leader must employ effective motivation. Motivation encourages employees, with reward incentives, to modify behavior and performance to reach a desired outcome. Motivation is a function of consequences. Consequences can be positive or negative. For example, employees who are motivated by money will complete tasks with the promise of financial gain. Conversely, think of an employee with a history of tardiness. The initial consequence may be a reprimand, or perhaps even suspension of pay, to deter further unwanted tardiness. This is a negative consequence; the ultimate goal is to motivate the employee to modify their behavior by reporting to work on time.

Motivations have evolved as generations have progressed. During the Great Depression, people were motived to put food on their tables to feed their families. As the nation became more prosperous, food scarcity and hunger declined. This ameliorated the need to work solely for food provisions and ushered in a new era of motivations. Motivations vary from person to person, and within the context of the current social and political climates.

Generation Z is motivated by time away from the workplace, to maintain a healthy work-life balance. In my own experience, productivity increased when employees were incentivized with additional time away from the workplace. This can be accomplished with creative scheduling and a focus on positive consequence, versus negative or punitive consequence. Moreover, nurturing this work-life balance not only increases productivity, but further bolsters morale.

It is essential to know and understand your employees in order to implement the correct motivational tool. As was learned in earlier chapters, Generation Z employees have a strong desire to own their own companies. They also want to have a direct impact on the organization for which they work. Utilizing this information, a leader needs to develop a motivational plan in which desired behaviors or benchmarks result in increased voice in the decision making processes of the organization.

CHAPTER SEVEN
Work Groups

With internet growth since the mid-1990's, the influence of online markets has increased dramatically. Content creators and social influencers started filling that online space. This shift to digital content creation allowed people to more easily become independent and entrepreneurial. Generation Z experienced this change during their youth, empowering them to become their own boss. Employee desire to be in charge is a common trait that is loathed by managers. This is often misinterpreted as young employees wanting to do what they want, rather than a young entrepreneurial spirit.

Being able to harness that spirit and empower the next generation to think independently, and sometimes disagree with the status quo, can lead to tremendous growth, if implemented correctly. Millennials desired working hand-in-hand. Generation Z, however, prefers independent work that contributes to a more collaborative effort. As leaders, we must show how their roles fit into the broader landscape of the organization. In doing so, Generation Z employees will have greater buy in and allegiance to the company.

For example, to involve Generation Z employees in the decision making process and the company's larger picture, allow them to participate in meetings to which they may not have been previously privy to. Additionally, give them authority to work through their problems independently. Do not dictate specific tasks. This fosters critical and global thinking. These strategies, by increasing buy-in, ultimately lead to greater productivity.

One of the quickest ways to build trust in an employee is to show them that you value their opinion. By giving your employees the authority to make decisions as well as the autonomy to carry out their choices, you build trust and commitment. As leaders, we have to understand that our first job is to lead other people up to our level. The only way to do that is to delegate authority and autonomy.

One of the most successful programs I have ever run in

my office was developed entirely by a Generation Z employee. The managerial staff thought I was crazy to give authority and autonomy to this young employee. I presented a specific problem to the employee with the associated research data. I gave the employee full autonomy to interpret the information and develop a plan of action. Allowing the employee to work through the problem independently and recruit and collaborate with other employees as needed yielded a rapid increase in productivity as well as a solution to the problem.

Through this exercise, I was able to give my employees a sense of ownership. That empowered them to become more active and engaged in the organization's overall mission. They started thinking like leaders rather than entry-level employees.

Remember as a leader, our Generation Z employees, while new, are a valuable asset. As supervisors, we need to trust them. If we do not trust them, we should not have hired them. We cannot forget that we valued their opinions during the interview process which spurred on their employment. Expect your new employees to make mistakes. Use those errors as opportunities to coach, guide, and mentor them for future growth. Remember when you give feedback, to keep it short and in-person as to avoid any miscommunication.

Review: Work Groups:

- Create a collaborative environment.

- Show how an assigned task fits into a larger end-goal.

- Invite young employees to meetings and work-groups.

- Value employee opinions.

- Give autonomy as well as authority to implement new ideas.

CHAPTER EIGHT
Time Away

Generation Z values life outside of work more than any prior generation. Baby Boomers placed importance on time at work to fund their lifestyles. The more they worked, the more they could afford to fund their personal and professional identities. Millennials, and even more so Generation Z, place emphasis on life independent of their careers. Money is no longer the primary motivator for Generation Z rather a healthy work and life balance is.

That observation alone is enough to point us to a motivation tactic for a Generation-Z employee. Previous generations were motivated extrinsically by the promise of financial gains such as overtime or bonuses. Generation-Z is more engaged by being afforded opportunities such as working from home. As a leader it is essential to long-term success to know what motivates people.

For example, when faced with a difficult project, it is okay to ask your employees to put in more time and effort. However, it is important to balance give and take. Take your employees time and effort; give them something that appeals to their needs. Generation Z values more time away from work. Therefore, once they have put in the extra time and effort to complete the project, give them additional time away from work. One way of accomplishing this is to develop a schedule that affords them the opportunity to take off from work without utilizing vacation hours. A traditional 8-hours per day, 5-days per week work week can be adjusted to a 10-hours per day, 4-day work week. This frees up an additional day for your employee to have to themselves which can feel like added time away from work.

When this tactic was employed in my workplace, the results were astounding. Not only did employees work above expectations, one employee even booked a cruise during his additional time-off. Affording employees time away from work also allows them to mentally recharge and enjoy a healthier work-life balance. Employees were happier with more perceived time off, while getting more work done. Furthermore, this practice not only led to increased productivity, but also an increase in morale. Funny enough, the more accommodating the workplace became, the more the employees wanted to be at work.

A critical component of succeeding in this type of flexible time-management is having frank conversations with employees. Explain expectations and hold employees accountable. For example, objectively measure productivity. If your goal demands increased productivity and an employee is not meeting the predetermined goal, do not reward that employee with time away from work. If an employee tries to take advantage of this opportunity, explain why their actions are insufficient and perhaps withhold the opportunity for a set amount of time. For example, a former employee attempted to extort this time off opportunity. After a frank conversation about inadequate productivity and a two month penalty period, his productivity skyrocketed as he saw the value and joy other employees experienced from flexible scheduling. The motivating factor for him was that he had a wife and two young children at home. The fewer days he spent at work, the more time he could spend at home with his family.

Review: Time Away

- Seek flexible work hour opportunities.

- Value a healthy work/life balance.

- Explain and set expectations.

- Provide frequent feedback to performance.

CHAPTER NINE
Building Trust

Trust is paramount in any organization, yet delicate. Trust must be a two-way street, both up and down the hierarchy of an organization. How can leaders gain the trust of Generation-Z? Generation-Z places a lot of trust in social media influencers. This is because social media influencers are relatable and give honest reviews. If Generation-Z trusts a person, they will listen intently upon what they have to say and follow their recommendations.

To gain the trust of Generation Z, you must look at how they give their confidence to others. Simply opening Instagram and clicking the trending tab provides valuable insight. They watch 30 to 60-second videos of influencers who are being genuine. This brief yet recurrent interaction reinforces the viewers trust in the influencer.

In practicality, these short videos provide a blueprint to build trust with your Generation-Z employees. These videos suggest that informally meeting with people fosters trust, which can be recreated in the workgroup. They can be viewed as a way to informally meet with people and build trust amongst the workgroup. Instead of creating an Instagram page, make Instagram a real-world experience. Much like the principle "Lead by walking around," perhaps bring people together over coffee.

Think back in your career: When was the last time the boss took time out of his or her day to meet with employees? As a formal leader, I did just that. One day I picked up my cup of coffee, I walked into coworking office, and sat down. There was no agenda, or official business to discuss. I talked about life, similar to what social influencers do every day. We talked sports, family, and current events. There was no science, it was just me genuinely getting to know people.

Over time the boss-employee dynamic shifted from fear to trust. Previously, a visit from the boss meant that someone was in trouble. As frequent, informal meetings continued, fear began to fade away. Employees began looking forward to when I would show up in their space with coffee in hand. They even started an office pool to get higher-end coffee than what was typically served in the break room. They began calling it the coffee club, getting different varieties of coffee, brewing it and sharing with me. We were almost becoming coffee connoisseurs. I was gaining their trust, one cup of coffee at a time.

Over time, the employees felt more comfortable discussing not only their weekend plans, but also organizational improvements. Some of their ideas were fantastic. The solutions they suggested were enacted as quickly as possible that were within my span of control. Some of their suggestions had been unsuccessfully tried in the past, so an explanation as to why a particular idea did not work was offered. Providing feedback made them feel that even though I was saying no to their idea, I was at least hearing them out.

As these meetings continued, trust increased and productivity continued to increase. The trust we built increased morale and motivation. Other managers were incorporated into the daily coffee sessions. Employees began to trust the leaders of the organization and therefore the organization itself. As we shared visions for the organizations future, the employees completed on-thespot problem-solving about how to achieve the vision.

A secondary benefit of these meetings was that employees were starting to think like managers. Rather than thinking as entry level employees, they began understanding how their role fit into the organization's global landscape. Metaphorically, instead of placing a brick in a wall, they were building a cathedral. They were starting to take even more ownership for the organization.

The coffee meetings only lasted five to 10 minutes each day, but they proved invaluable for improving the employees' morale, productivity, and overall mental well-being. We changed the mindset from fear of the boss to viewing the position as an approachable mentor. As I shared more organizational information with them, they reciprocated. They became better followers and better leaders by merely having more of a vested interest in the organization.

As leaders, we must understand that hierarchy exists to pass information. Directives are usually doled out from the top level and pushed down to the bottom. Sometimes the things that are missed in the process is how a directive affects the person actually completing the task. By opening the line of communication and fostering trust, we were able to discuss, redefine and accomplish new goals to move the organization forward. Collaboration yielded better outcomes than what I would have conceived on my own.

Review: Building Trust:

- *Be genuine.*

- *Create informal meetings, in a space that is comfortable for the employee.*

- *Informal meetings lead to organizational solutions.*

- *Value employee ideas and implement change when possible.*

Inspire.

CHAPTER TEN
Inspire.

To be inspirational, a leader must know his or her employees. One of the best things a leader can do is invest in employees. Putting in time and energy to honestly know and understand your people will provide immense benefits in the long term. A leader must understand an employee's background because that impacts the employee's decision making process. Once you understand, you can influence. You can lead. When you have the ability to lead, you have the ability to motivate. Inspiration comes as a culmination of understanding, leading, and motivating. To inspire is to give an innate sense of purpose.

CHAPTER ELEVEN
Advocate for Others

To determine what inspires Generation-Z, insight is gained by viewing current movie trends and the evening news. This is the generation that created anti-bullying campaigns, organized donation drives for the less-fortunate, and leveraged the power of social media to enact social change. The culture is shifting away from backstabbing and cut-throat tactics for personal gain. The culture is evolving to promote advocacy and altruism in the everyday.

In the past, the stereotypical teenager possessed a self-serving attitude. They were represented in pop-culture as scheming to get ahead at every turn. Bullying was almost standard practice. That stereotype showed up in print, film, and radio so often that it seemed like a fact of life. Think of the movie *Sixteen Candles* or more recent films such as

Mean Girls or *American Pie*. Each of these films depicted a stereotype of youth corresponding to the generation in which they were produced. The youth grew up and became Millennials. That was the culture they lived in and experienced. Millennials viewed growing up as almost a rite of passage, trying to fit in at each turn. In earlier generations, school was seen as a social proving-ground in which traits were learned that carried us into adulthood.

As time has changed, so have the mindsets of the generations. The transition started with Millennials, with tolerance and social advocacy. Generation-Z has continued this evolution. These generations embrace advocacy for other people. Anti-bullying campaigns and acceptance crusades top the headlines. The next generation is coming of age in a world in which everyday people fought for same-sex marriage legalization, pushed for climate change legislation, and tackled minority rights issues head-on. Even though these are relatively new topics, the teenagers during these times are set to turn 23 years old in 2020. We are already seeing them enter the workforce. Generation-Z employees are accustomed to this world of advocacy.

How can a leader use this to his or her advantage? The

answer is simple. Be an advocate for your employees. Think of your workplace as a function of human nature. We are social creatures, and as such we form social groups. When a leader pays close attention to the social roles within the work environment, he or she can gain incredible insight into informal social hierarchies. Additionally, there are informal social leaders as well as liaisons who interact with many different workplace cliques simultaneously. This is where a leader can use the art of advocacy to their advantage.

To build trust and group cohesion, advocate for your employees with your employees. A leader must be genuine and unsolicited. Conversing in a break room and speaking positively about one employee or several employees fosters buy-in. This not only benefits those who are listening, but also the employees being referenced. Thus, employees' positive traits are brought to the forefront which ultimately creates a more positive workplace culture. Take the time to learn your employees' traits and engage with the current events affecting them.

As a leader, chatting with members of different social circles is beneficial. Groups interact with one another and share information despite being seemingly isolated from each other. In other words, people talk. The best example of this is the dreaded "rumor mill." We can all think of a time when a person said or did something which then spread throughout the entire office.

In the past, I took over a work unit of 17 people, with whom I had not previously worked. As colleagues inquired about my new role and how the workgroup was handling with a new formal leader, I ensured an intentional answer. I went by my grandmother's rule: If you don't have anything nice to say, don't say anything at all. In leadership, staying silent is not an option. Therefore, it is imperative that you say something positive about everyone. With each interaction, advocating for each employee was the goal.

I advocated heavily for my new team. I cited specific employee accomplishments and praised their combined successes. When meetings were held with other department heads, I knew my messages would eventually be communicated throughout various groups, and then back to my employees. The message to the new work group had to be clear; the formal leader valued them. That's not to say that underperforming employees were not held accountable. Those who were underperforming were counseled privately, however always praised publicly. As far as public perception was concerned, our workgroup was accomplishing amazing things and I was lucky to be part of it.

This communication technique is incredibly effective and necessary during periods of change. Positive affirmations via word-of-mouth feedback improve employee morale and performance. Think back to a time when you found out that your boss was singing your praises. How did that make you feel? You likely felt valued as an employee. Perhaps your buy-in to the company became stronger in that moment than it had been previously. When commitment increases, job performance and satisfaction increase.

Review: Advocate for Others:

- *Understand the dynamics of the informal workplace hierarchy.*

- *If you don't have anything nice to say, don't say anything at all.*

- *Notice positive actions performed by your employees.*

- *Support your employees the way you want to be supported.*

CHAPTER TWELVE
Continued Optimism

Millennials and Generation-Z value altruism in the workplace. These generations desire networking with others to accomplish tasks they would not be able to complete on their own. Generation-Z and Millennials still value happy hours at local watering holes. However, these generations are looking to utilize their networks to form bonds to create change in the world. They want to make a difference in the world by use of their corporate networks to pay it forward. They are thinking globally and acting locally.

According to the ADP Research Institute, social gatherings for Generation Z should include volunteer opportunities and charitable events[16]. Generation Z is interested in improving themselves as well as the lives of others. Social media is inundated with pictures of humanitarian endeavors such as mission trips to Haiti, ice bucket challenges, and volunteer events. There is a social pressure to do good which, creates a desire to participate. Generation-Z wants to work for companies that hold the same beliefs. The concept of having a purpose and giving back to communities is at the heart of the generation[17].

As leaders, we have the ability to foster an environment in which our employees thrive. Give employees the opportunity to serve mankind while at work. In order to accomplish this, you must show that you believe in something. Believe in something and do it with conviction. Offer up the chance for your team to come together and further a cause through fundraising, volunteering, or utilizing their social media savvy as a way to spread a

[16] **Turner, Marcia Layton. (2018).** "How Generation Z Views the Future: A Word on Optimism." *Spark.* Accessed March 26, 2019. https://www.adp.com/spark/articles/2018/12/how-generation-z-views-the-future-a-word-on-optimism.aspx#

[17] Ibid.

positive message. While these functions may or may not affect the company's bottom line, they offer amazing team-building opportunities and a way for team members to connect outside of the office.

In transformational leadership theory, the leader must align their philosophies to the group or the organization. The leaders task it to set an example and become the role model for the group. Be honest with your employees and identify values that they deem most important. Generation-Z wants to work for and with companies which improve the world. As leaders, we must not only embrace that idealistic philosophy, but live it.

Inspiring the workforce of today is a long-term response to global changes. As value systems change, so must our leadership styles. Giving back to the world and ensuring that all peoples, regardless of background, are included in our vision is the key to success. Lead with ideas, the people will follow.

Review: Continued Optimism:

- *Encourage altruistic efforts.*

- *Organize workplace volunteer groups.*

- *Act with conviction when championing for a cause.*

- *Encourage positive problem solving to global problems.*

CHAPTER THIRTEEN
Skill Building

Generation Z is often misconceived as a generation of "know-it-all's". As leaders, we must avoid this misconception. Not only is it far from the truth, it also sets lousy precedence and perpetuates a negative prejudice about an entire generation who do, in fact, know a lot.

Recently, I had the opportunity to sit in a roundtable discussion of employers and employees. Like most companies, employers are finding that old tactics no longer worked on the newest generation of employees. The roundtable was developed so that the leaders of the organization could meet with their youngest employees and develop new strategies on how to inspire them. As I observed, I was amazed by the young employee's responses. Not because they were stating things that were new, profound, or earth-shattering. Rather, I was pleasantly surprised that their reactions, questions, comments, and concerns aligned perfectly with current Generation-Z data.

Not once did any of them allude to "knowing everything." The Gen Z'ers had quite the opposite tone. They repeatedly stated sentiments such as, "I know I have a lot to learn," or "I'm still developing my knowledge." In fact, they craved more knowledge.

What they did speak about was the need to develop themselves further. The Generation-Z employees expressed a lack of mentorship, informal leadership, and coaching in the workplace. They yearned for skill-building, even at an entry level position. They wanted lower-level supervisors orienting and guiding them to build their confidence in what they were doing.

Additionally, they expressed concern about insufficient feedback from supervisors. They quoted managers as answering the age-old question of, "Why do we do it this way?" with the most dreaded answer, "Because we have always done it this way." They weren't asking the question to be difficult. Remember, Generation-Z seeks to understand and desires frequent feedback. They ask questions because they care about how their role fits into the organization and how that impacts their career development.

Generation Z is accustomed to constant feedback. As leaders, we can capitalize on Generation-Z employees by implementing mentoring strategies with frequent communication. Generation-Z wants to know what they are doing right and what they are doing wrong. Spend time with your people and build them up. This generation is the future; eventually they will replace all of us as organizational leaders. We owe it to them, our organizations, and ourselves to continually develop future leaders.

Part of skill building is global understanding. Allowing a Generation-Z employee to shadow an employee from a different part of the organization can lead to a more well-rounded workforce. This allows for a "big-picture" mentality while simultaneously introducing fresh ideas into the status quo. We are all shaped by our experiences; the more experiences we have, the better equipped we are to navigate multiple situations.

Do not discount members of Generation Z simply based on age. They are the most educated generation to have ever walked the planet with nearly 70 percent of high school graduates enrolling in a college or university a rate which has steadily increased over the past two decades. [18]They are an incredibly intelligent and adaptable group. They are aware that they have a lot to learn. They are also incredibly eager to learn. Generation Z not only wants to do their jobs, but they also want to understand how their jobs fit into the larger organization, to ultimately make the organization stronger.

---

[18] **National Center for Educational Statistics. (2019).** Enrollment Facts. Accessed September 26, 2019. https://nces.ed.gov/fastfacts/display.asp?id=98

Review: Skill Building:

- *Understand that Gen-Z'ers self identify as needing to learn.*

- *Develop coaching and mentoring relationships.*

- *Do not dictate with mandates.*

- *Critically analyze why processes and procedures were developed.*

- *Be open to change in written policies and procedures.*

'They' Are Not Millennials

As society rapidly evolves, so must the leaders. If we continue to discount groups of people just because we do not understand them, we are wrong. We are wrong for stereotyping Millennials just as we are wrong for not seeing the differences between generations of employees including Generation Z and Millennials. Leadership is fluid. When something no longer works, it is incumbent upon the leader to analyze the situation and develop a new plan. Simply throwing in the towel is not an option.

At the end of the day, there are certain constants we can fall back on. The first is that leadership is the art and science of getting others to do what you need them to do. The second is that we are all humans, with our own unique traits, but can grow into new people over time.

As you continue your own personal leadership journey,

remember it is not about you. It is always about the people you lead.

Bibliography

Gallup, Inc. 2016. "2017 National Scorecard." Accessed March 26, 2019. http://www.gallupstudentpoll.com/197492/2016-national-scorecard.aspx.

Lingo Staffing. 2018. "Generation Z is Here: Is Your Company Ready for the New Kids on the Workforce Block?" Accessed March 26, 2019. https://lingostaffing.com/1091-2/.

Geyser, Werner. 2019. "Why YouTube Stars are More Influential than Traditional Celebrities." Influencer Marketing Hub. Accessed March 26, 2019. https://influencermarketinghub.com/youtube-stars-influential-traditional-celebrities/..

Brenner, Michael. 2014. "Thanks Social Media - Our Average Attention Span Is Now Shorter Than Goldfish." Marketing Insider Group.Accessed March 26, 2019. https://marketinginsidergroup.com/content-marketing/thanks-social-media-average-attention-span-now-shorter-goldfish/

Gelber, Mack. 2016. "Here's what you need to know about Gen Z, boss." **Monster Career Advice.** Accessed March 26, 2019. https://www.monster.com/career-advice/article/gen-z-boss-0816

National Center for Educational Statistics. 2019. "Fast Facts: Enrollment." Accessed September 26, 2019. https://nces.ed.gov/fastfacts/display.asp?id=98

Patel, Deep. 2017. "How Gen Z Will Affect The Future Of The Peer To Peer Economy."*Forbes*.https://www.forbes.com/sites/deeppatel/2017/08/29/how-gen-z-will-affect-the-future-of-the-peer-to-peer-economy/.

* * *

Perez, Sarah. 2018. "Twitter's doubling of character count from 140 to 280 had little impact on length of tweets." *TechCrunch*. Accessed March 26, 2019. https://techcrunch.com/2018/10/30/twitters-doubling-of-character-count-from-140-to-280-had-little-impact-on-length-of-tweets/.

Pew Research Center: Internet and Technology. (2014). "Part 1: How the internet has woven itself into American life." Accessed March 26, 2019. https://www.pewinternet.org/2014/02/27/part-1-how-the-internet-has-woven-itself-into-american-life/.

Turner, Marcia Layton. (2018). "How Generation Z Views the Future: A Word on Optimism." *Spark*. Accessed March 26, 2019. https://www.adp.com/spark/articles/2018/12/how-generation-z-views-the-future-a-word-on-optimism.aspx#

Stahl, Ashley. (2017). "Why Democrats Should be Losing Sleep Over Generation Z. *Forbes*. Accessed March 26, 2019. https://www.forbes.com/sites/ashleystahl/2017/08/11/why-democrats-should-be-losing-sleep-over-generation-z/#55fe57657878

About the Author

David Brown is a millennial in a leadership position. When he is not researching generational differences he can be found at his day job with the Ohio State Highway Patrol. David instructs leadership development at the Patrol's training academy. He can be contacted at www.davidbrownonline.com.

'They' Are Not Millennials

www.ingramcontent.com/pod-product-compliance
Lightning Source LLC
Chambersburg PA
CBHW030530210326
41597CB00014B/1100